Dragonfly Wings
A Collection of Memories

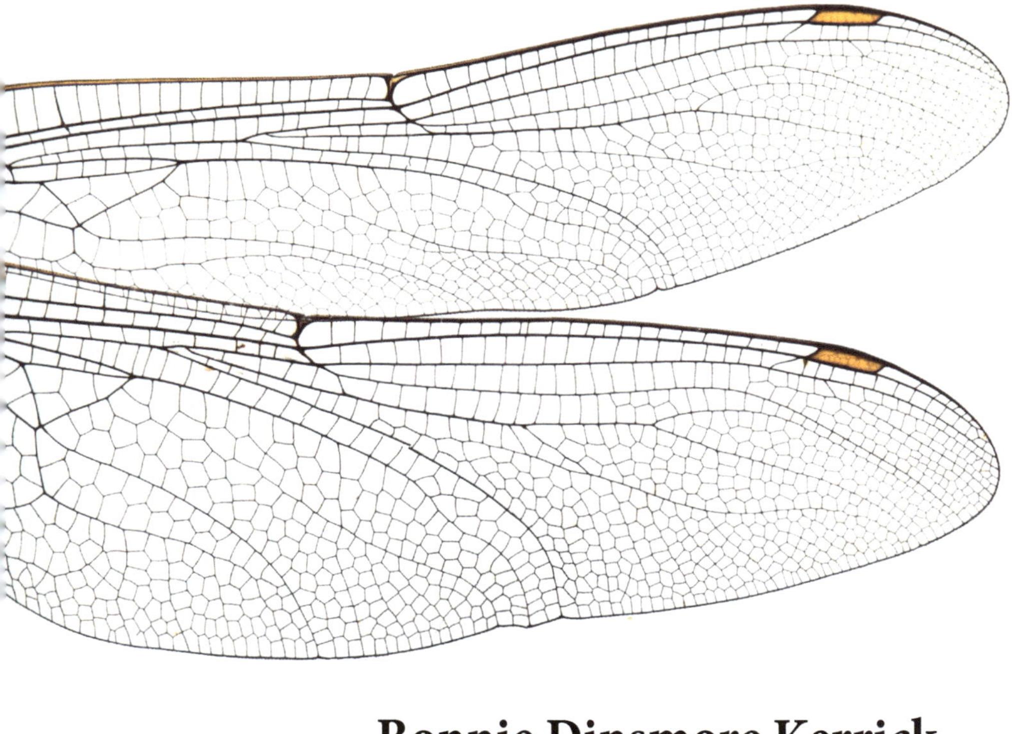

Bonnie Dinsmore Kerrick

Dragonfly Wings
Copyright 2017 by Bonnie Dinsmore Kerrick
All Rights Reserved. Please do not reproduce without the permission of the author. It is believed that all images within this book are public domain. If you believe this is not the case, please contact the publisher at the address below.

Published by Piscataqua Press
142 Fleet St.
Portsmouth, NH
03801
www.piscataquapress.com

ISBN: 978-1-944393-54-0

Printed in the United States

FOR COURTNEY

and her boys, Brodi and Teagan

Very special thanks to my dear friends, Dorothy Spelman (editing), and Barb Jenny (design) for their exceptional contributions to this book!

You guys rock!!

The Flame

The flame burst forth
Long after it should have
But -no matter- It glowed with an intensity
That belied its latent inception
As if wanting to catch up
To all the other flames
It filled the room with brilliance
Long after many other flames had sputtered to their end
Then, quite suddenly, it flickered
Wavering between eternity and extinction
Then died, struggling against the commitment
But the wax that had given it life
Remained warm and soft

Philadelphia, 1962

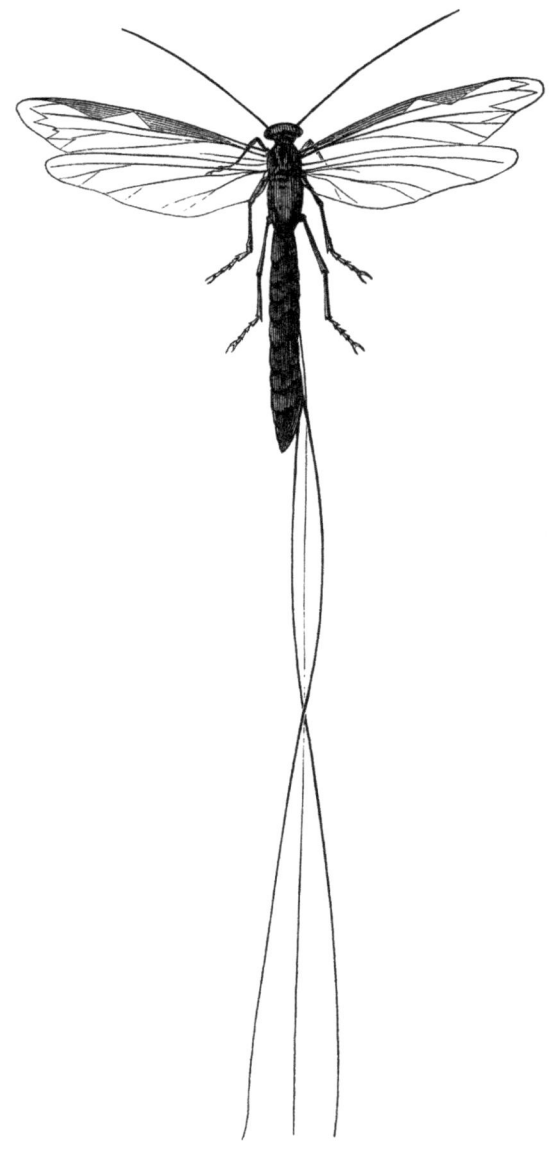

Kirk

We've come so far along this road
I thought we were a pair
And I'm the one who's turning back
To leave you standing there
How strange it is, for I had thought
It would be the other way 'round
But you're still walking in the sand
And I want firmer ground
The fog lifts from behind us
But ahead the air is gray
I wish we'd find another road
And then perhaps I'd stay
But I'll go back and rest a while
I'm weary from the walk
Perhaps you will grow weary, too
And then, perhaps, we'll talk

Philadelphia, 1965

Camp Nurse Farewell – Tall Timbers

The making of speeches for me is a ruse
So I've borrowed an idea from old Dr. Seuss
Instead of orating an old epic tome
I've decided to send you all home with a poem
A poem…you say…why…a poem about me?
This girl is crazy, how can this thing be?
Well, if you've been seen for some itches or scratches
Or used my peroxide or band-aids or patches
Then this poem is for you, sir, you see it applies
To almost every single one of you guys
I've dropped in your ears and your eyes and your noses
My medicine's covered your heads and your toe-ses
With Caladryl, Benadryl, ointments and lotions
Donnatal, Cepacol -magical potions
Some boys were eager and some were unwillin'
Some got to gargle, some took penicillin
Some noses bled and some just got stuffy
Some ankles got sore and some ankles got puffy
I know all your names and I know all your faces
I know when you've hurt and I know in which places
And now it's good-bye to your sniffles and sneezes
And stomach aches, head aches, sore muscles, and wheezes
I've had a fine summer, I hope you have too
And without further comment, I bid you adieu!

Casco, ME 1966

Going Away

Going away is hard
When everyone loves you
And you love them
And the life you've been building is comfortable and safe

Going away is easy
When you find you're bored
And take those you love for granted
And you've stopped building a life and started digging a hole

Going away hurts
Because you only take yourself
And it's all so new and strange
And you never imagined you'd feel so alone

Going away feels good
When you realize you're OK on your own
And you have people to miss
And lots of people don't

Denver 1967

On My Way

I've got to see the rivers while they're full of melted snow
I've got to see the ocean in the rain
I've got to see the mountains overwhelm the countryside
I've got to leave you on the morning train

The cactus growing spiney as it reaches to the sky
The breeze that brings the new mown grass to mind
The laughter of the children as they tumble in the snow
For all of this I must leave you behind

The silent streams are whispering over silent mossy rocks
I have to go and hear the tale they tell
Such beauty won't replace the tender moments in your arms
But you and I both know me far too well

Culver Lake, 1965

Emerging

The restlessness you feel inside
Comes on when you might least expect
It surges slowly into mind
Until it grabs you by the neck
It turns your head this way and that
And conjures up a million dreams
You thought you had so well repressed
By lakes well fed by mountain streams
You wonder at the mountains high
The cool clear babbling of the brook
You worry and consider why
You never read a hundred books
Why not, the trip you never took
The jobs in cities for away
Why weren't things then as they are now
And why for God's sake did you stay?

Philadelphia, 1966

Heritage | J.B.W.D

You lousy drunk

I have your eyes

I have your smile

Reluctantly I swim in your gene pool treading water

I have your smile

I have your eyes

You lousy drunk

Philadelphia, 1966

CWK

I can't make the time stop
But I can make a teardrop
For every single moment we're apart
I can't make it hurtless
Because I was so heartless
And you and I can't go back to the start

So much of growing up is pain
Into my life comes so much rain
I wonder if I'll ever see the sun
You taught me how to care, love
You taught me how to share, love
I wish that I could end what has begun

I've never felt this way before
You've opened up a brand new door
Your love has given birth to something new
I am so down, I must look up
I've tasted something from life's cup
And now I'm losing me and losing you

We had a part but not the whole
I knew that deep within my soul
That ours was not a love to weather time
I know we both will love again
I can't imagine where or when
But when we do I know it will be fine

Time will heal all wounds they say
Cheer up, you'll see a brighter day
Why don't they understand the hurt's inside
I've waited for this love too long
And now it's ruined, it's gone wrong
I don't know what to show and what to hide

Denver, 1967

Nature/Nurture

I never felt you kick and move against me in my belly
For those nine months we waited for you to be born
But I have felt you kick and move against my heart
For these 28 years you have been becoming you

When you were four days old, I held you in my arms for the first time
And I became the one you would kick and move against for all your life
I wasn't there when you were growing into a baby
But when you came screaming out
Into the world you were mine, and I was yours

No umbilical cord held you to me, so I forged one with love, patience,
More love, and my incredibly strong belief in you
You grew out of my soul like you grew out of her womb
You are my child ...of her...of me... but most important, now, of yourself
There is no feeling like this...to see you so grown up from all this time and struggle
Out of her womb...out of my love... into your own life

Cambridge, 2001

The Awakening

Honking geese
Swept along on the freshening wind
Herald its arrival
Tree roots beneath the earth
Stretch and drink
Long dormant earthworms
Extend and contract
In the softening soil

Verdant hillsides
Proudly boast
Brilliant washes of yellow and pink
Tender shoots
Erupting from the moist earth
Test the constancy of the warming sun

Mountain streams
Gorged with melted snow
Dance swiftly over slippery rocks
Once again
Mother Nature awakens
And is renewed

Cambridge 2002

Therapy

My life for moments, hours, in your hands
What to remember
What to forget
Clarity and confusion
Joy and pain
But always your presence
Helping

Written for Betsey Edwards, May 2004

Heritage II | F.W.D.

My father's brother gives me things
My father never could
Like family pride and true self worth
And all things that are good
I hold my head up higher now
Because of course I should

Brookline, 2005

Craig

Husband, dad, friend, colleague

Love flows from you

Like a quiet deep spring

Nourishing all

Cape Neddick, 2010

What Remains

What remains of my vibrant, gregarious, larger-than-life mother
Is about three cups of mostly fine gray ash
Confined in a heavy-duty plastic bag within a white sturdy cardboard box
She seems discarded—an afterthought of afterlife
I move her to a Tupperware container with a bright red top
And paste on colorful Winnie-the-Pooh stickers
A friendlier and happy place for her repose
Until we toss her ashes this summer into her
Beloved Culver Lake
But then I add several thimbles-full of her into a sterling silver
Tiffany pill box and I know this is where she can be truly
Comfortable and at rest
And there she will stay with me forever

Cape Neddick, May 8, 2006

Media Medusa

Your serpent tongues

Taste the desires of our youth

And spit back venom

Cambridge, 2003

www.ingramcontent.com/pod-product-compliance
Lightning Source LLC
Chambersburg PA
CBHW041756040426
42446CB00001B/56